Emergence
by Hayli Nicole

Copyright © 2019 Hayli Nicole
www.haylinicole.com

Cover and interior design by the author
Printed and bound in the United States of America

First edition printed May 12, 2019
The color edition printed November 12, 2019
This edition published February 20, 2020

All rights reserved. No part of this publication may be reproduced, stored in a retrieval system, or transmitted in any form or by any means, electronic, mechanical, photocopying, recording, or otherwise without prior permission of the copyright owner.

Paperback Editions
ISBN: 978-0-9966711-0-1 (Black & White)
ISBN: 978-0-9966711-9-4 (Color)

Self-published by Hayli Nicole
Legasis Publishing
www.projectlegasis.com

*Dedicated to Carrie
for believing in
my early poetry
and teaching mindfulness
before it was
ever a thing.
My dear friend Jimmy
whose death inspired
a new direction
of living and
being more intentional
in the world.
And to Basile
for setting my soul
and creativity ablaze
the day
you came
into my life.*

Contents

Preface	ix
Jimmy	1
Genesis	5
Foundations	27
Emergence	49

Preface

This entire book can be blamed, if you will, on one man.

He is the reason I stepped out into the world and discovered the sides of myself I am now able to share transparently with others. He was the first person waiting with open arms upon my arrival home, eager to learn about places he never dreamed of experiencing himself. He sat with me in the dark corners of bars for late shifts, we shared the stage in the stand-up comedy scene, he worked tirelessly with me to build a successful entertainment company, he helped me articulate new dreams until they were well-rehearsed, and he never stopped supporting me even when time and physical distance were working against us.

He was the first person who ever believed in me as a writer and one of the only people I shared my poetry with. He is the reason I am able to stand confidently as the woman I know myself to be today, and I will forever consider him the first person who showed me how to embody a gracious heart.

Unfortunately, it took Jimmy's tragic death to finally have the courage to bring this book of poetry to life. In losing him, I was faced with the harsh realization I had become stagnant in the dreams he helped me create, so I worked on breathing life into them again. His death was the thing to bring me back into alignment with my creative goals and emerge the woman he always believed I could become.

This book is for Jimmy as a thank you for everything he did, and continues to do, for me in this life.

The poems are sorted into three sections: Genesis, Foundations, and Emergence. I've shared a few anecdotes as to why I settled on these words, which were heavily influenced and indirectly chosen by Jimmy.

Genesis includes my early poetry—as early as 2005 and spans through 2009. While the word Genesis has biblical affiliations for most, Jimmy redefined it for me one night while we were drinking stale coffee at Denny's.

It was 2012. Jimmy and I had met a few months prior while performing stand-up comedy. We frequented the same mics and quickly became attached at the hip. He was the first friend I made in adulthood, and I trusted him more than anyone else in my life. I was trying to figure out a name for the karaoke company I was about to purchase and he was helping bounce ideas around. Legacy was a prominent word for me at the time, but it didn't feel unique enough to what we were doing. This was the beginning of an unexpected life trajectory, and I wanted the name to be as unconventional as the decision was. That's when Jimmy suggested combining words.

We took legacy and genesis, meaning the beginning of something, and combined them to form Legasis. To us, this commitment meant the beginning of a shared legacy. For three years, he would help me operate the company as Legasis Entertainment. It opened some unexpected doors and introduced creative collaborations, which led to deep and meaningful relationships still influencing my life to this day. As I've continued to evolve through several business ventures, life transitions, and upheavals, genesis remains to be the confirmation that all dreams have to begin somewhere to become a legacy.

This book is every part of Jimmy's as it is my own.

While writing this collection, I found my first poetry journal from high school. Adolescence is tumultuous for just about everyone, but I have vivid memories of feeling like an outcast and constantly being bullied for things ultimately out of my control. I was searching for ways to express myself, so I experimented with poetry at the encouragement of my high school English teacher, Carrie, who I also dedicate this book.

I used the sticky notes Carrie, and later Jimmy, wrote in this journal to choose which poems to include in Genesis. They were the only people I trusted to read these vulnerable musings from my younger self, so it felt right to include their input. It was an interesting thing, revisiting what I wrote at a significantly broken stage of my life. As adults, I think we forget (or consciously suppress) how much pain we worked through during our formative years. Still, it's impossible to deny my inspiration came from experiencing such volatile emotions.

San Diego was at the mercy of savage wildfires, claiming the homes of friends (Mothers of Mayhem). I experienced my first tragic death—a drunk driving accident involving one of my peers (Sober, Drunk). Carrie introduced me to my favorite transcendentalists and how to write Shakespearean sonnets (Constellations, Kissed by a Rose). She also challenged me to write more prose with less structure, though that style wouldn't re-emerge until much later in life.

Immediately following high school, my parents went through a devastating divorce that spanned my first (and only) year living away at college. This led to reckless experimentation with drugs and alcohol, the dismantling of what little self-confidence I possessed and left me susceptible to forming codependent behaviors. This is also the period when I fell in love for the first time. While I was able to draw inspiration from our tumultuous six-year romance, our emotionally abusive relationship was the thing to extinguish my voice as a writer fully. It would be several years before I was inspired to write poetry again.

The poems included in Foundations were written between 2015 and 2018. I was struggling to find my place in the world and doubted my potential as a writer. I still found magic in the mundane, but poetry was the farthest thing from my mind. I knew writing was still rooted in my identity, but I had no idea how to use it to connect with the people in my life or my surroundings. I felt voiceless in a loquacious world but had so much I wanted to say. It turns out, the voice I considered lost was still within me after all. It merely needed immersive travels and creative exploration as its foundation to finally emerge.

Mother Nature (September 2015) was the first time I felt aligned with my dreams. I sold everything I owned, including the entertainment company, to pursue a volunteer opportunity to study orangutans in the wild. I remember sitting in the Sumatran rainforest after our first encounter with a subadult male. I was relaxing on a massive boulder in the middle of the river near our base camp. Trees towered around me in every direction with an impenetrable density. Cicadas were humming in perfect pitch, and the birds were highly active despite remaining unseen in the canopies. I remember feeling so unimportant at this moment—that every heartache and point of contention in my life was insignificant in the grand scheme of this earthly existence. I emerged from the rainforest a different person than when I entered. I had discovered this sense of freedom and wildness that propelled me into new experiences. I spent the next four months traveling through Indonesia, Cambodia, Malaysia, and Vietnam. Through the process of shedding what no longer served me, rooting myself in nature, and becoming more connected to cultures I once considered foreign, I returned to the States with a clearer vision of the future I dreamed for myself.

Except love would be the thing to derail said dreams—albeit temporarily. I blindly followed this love even if it meant living in a concrete jungle that nearly decimated the spirit I worked so hard to free. Because of a sexual assault in Cambodia, my days in San Francisco were plagued by panic attacks and PTSD. We found ways to travel together, which appeased my itchy feet and allowed me to catch my breath but living in the city was draining me of my emotional and physical well-being. It felt like I was constantly drowning in a place I knew I didn't belong. So, when an opportunity to move to Ireland presented itself the following year, we did what any two sane kids would do. We silently eloped and moved our entire lives abroad in a matter of weeks.

Ireland felt like life was finally on track. I was exploring the city and the beautiful countryside on weekends, making friends byway of my new husband. The newness of everything inspired the deepest parts of me. My spousal visa meant I wasn't legally allowed to work in Ireland, but I was writing full-time, which was the dream. We had a beautiful apartment with high ceilings and original crown molding in a desirable part of town. People believed in our love, and it felt good to finally feel supported. From the outside, our lives appeared to be perfect, but without the internal support from my husband, it was only a matter of time before the facade of our relationship crumbled.

Our proximity to Europe meant we were plotting adventures to new destinations almost weekly. I fell madly in love with our always being gone, which meant I fell into depression every time I was stuck at home. I found myself staring at the same four walls with no real routine. I had nothing of my own to show up for, so I stopped showing up for and taking care of myself. My only identity was an extension of his, and I became a shadow following in the footsteps of his experiences. By the end of the year, I found myself in the thick of winter depression, planning and paying for a second wedding I never wanted but was wholly for his benefit. I was becoming more detached the further I fell into my role as a housewife, maintaining an image for the benefit of everyone else but at the expense of my individuality. Our lives appeared to be a fairy tale, but I felt like a prisoner to the narrative I personally wrote into existence. The process of domestication was slowly suffocating me, and I lost all sense of purpose.

I was even beginning to lose the will to live.

When Jimmy died in June of 2018, the entire world went grey. I doubted I would ever see life the same again. I had become so detached from my being; it was easy to go through the motions of another tragic loss. After witnessing the outpouring of love at his funeral and a serendipitous introduction to Reiki, something within me changed. It felt as though life snapped back into alignment. Life quickly evolved into something far greater than anything I could have expected. I didn't know it, but I was about to embark on a spiritual journey beyond my comprehension.

With my husband's prior permission, I planned for a

quick return to Southeast Asia in August. After losing Jimmy, I extended my itinerary to span four months. I set the intention of reconnecting with the people who shaped (and saved) me in my previous travels. I was tired of being alone, so I vowed to share my adventures with as many humans as possible.

Before the big departure, I traveled to Scotland to reconnect with a friend I met while living in Sumatra. Returning to him felt like returning home, and I knew the rainforest would be the final piece to my healing journey. I wrote my first poem (The Highlands) in three years and realized life was about to come full-circle in myriad ways. When I ended up in Sri Lanka at the same time as a woman I knew from London, I was eager to trust the fortuitous alignment. We feared our fierce independence would cause us to quarrel, but our interests matched our strides, and we fell into perfect harmony. I was finding my humans and feeling at home in the world again.

I headed to Australia to reconnect with a couple I met bartending on a deserted island in Cambodia. They were the people I was with on the night of my assault, though I never had the courage to tell them. Their generosity is also the reason I was able to afford to buy a motorbike in Vietnam. Seeing them was another full-circle moment so vital to my healing.

We started in Melbourne, flew north to explore the sacred grounds of Uluru, and fulfilled my dream of driving along the Great Ocean Road. After so many years of silence, I finally told them what happened the night we parted ways at the bar in the small expat town of Kampot. Though there was a palpable weight to what was said, the unconditional love they showed me in this moment of truth finally freed me from the one thing that destroyed me.

Saying goodbye was bittersweet, but thirteen souls were waiting for me in Bali. We met on a photography tour in Iceland six months prior, and I had been working all summer to orchestrate our reunion. After a blissful week of morning meditations and creative collaborations, eight of them followed me to Bukit Lawang for a trek that would change all of our lives.

Returning to the rainforest was like stepping into a vortex.

The woman I was when I first entered, the woman I thought I lost and had been fighting my way back to, was the same woman I was when I emerged for a second time. It was as though I left her by the river to keep her safe knowing the devastation the next three years would entail. It felt as if no time had passed, only that I needed to return to find her again.

I filled three journals during the four months I was gone. The poems I curated for this section were written while grounding myself in nature, letting go of past lovers (Someday), exploring new lands, meditating regularly (Shwedagon), healing from sexual trauma, understanding the power of feminine energy (Cosmic Siren's Song), and finding new soulmates in far corners of the world (Under the Burmese Sun). Every missing piece of my healing journey fell perfectly into place. Life came full circle for me in extraordinary ways. Opportunities continued to align, leading me on a different life trajectory than intended when I first left.

When I returned to Ireland in November, life had taken on a different meaning. I refused to fall back into old routines. I could no longer remain still for life had become too precious. How could I waste my potential after feeling the repercussions of death? The months-long exploration of self and the insistence of following my dreams was met with discouragement and resistance from the one person who vowed to support me. It felt like I had to choose between the freedom to discover my true purpose and resuming my role as a lonely housewife.

Ultimately, I chose freedom.

The final section, Emergence, is a celebration of everything leading to the publication of this first book. It is the culmination of every dream I have seen manifest thus far, and the ones I know are waiting for me on the horizon. It is in honor of the people I will no longer have a chance to share this life with, as well as the people who have yet to align. Emergence is honoring the woman I was in the past and embracing the person I am eager to become in the future. But first, a story.

When I was still living in San Diego in 2014, Jimmy, myself, and our best friend David were at a showcase of mixed performing arts in Vista, California. We were the comedy portion of the lineup and were feeling quite intimidated by the insane talent we were sharing the microphone with that evening. Jimmy expected to be devoured alive because of his timid stature and one-liners, but I assured him they would love him.

After watching a particularly passionate piece of spoken word poetry, I leaned into Jimmy and told him one of my dreams was to perform but had no idea how to begin.

He said, "Hayli. If anyone can do spoken word, it's you."

After his quick nod of encouragement, I watched him destroy the room with his punny one-liners and quick bits of self-deprecation. It was rare to see him beaming after a set, but he didn't stop smiling. I saw in him the same thing he saw within me; the potential to make a difference in people's moods just by being your authentic, unabashed self. My only wish, even still, was that he could see in himself what was so apparent to the rest of us—how effortlessly talented and deeply loved he was by everyone.

It took five years from that night and the momentum of his loss, but in my final days of living in Ireland, I finally braved the stage of a poetry open mic. Dublin is immensely supportive of its artists and performers, so I felt immediately at home in the spoken word community. After my second night performing, I accepted an opportunity to feature the following week. I only had two poems at the time, but I needed enough material to fill 15 minutes. This meant feverishly writing for the next seven days despite the need to pack all of my earthly possessions for the international move home. There was something within me that poured rather effortlessly, and I blame the sudden surge of creativity on Jimmy.

These poems won't read the same as the previous ones, but through the process of performing what I've written, I have emerged the poet I always hoped I would become. It is the direction I know my poetry will continue to evolve and something I hope Jimmy will be proud of. I chose to end this collection with a poem I wrote about leaving Dublin—a place I called home for the better part of two years—and the simultaneous ending of my marriage. While it is clear now I was never meant to remain in one place, in setting temporary roots, I was able to lay the foundations to ignite this creative flame and emerge a woman fierce in her identity as a writer and as a poet.

This small book of poetry ended up being a much-needed introspection of my evolution through the years. Both personally and creatively, I have pursued some unconventional dreams, and they've led me further than where I hoped I would end up. While I have no idea where my journey will lead, I can't help but acknowledge every person and everything that has led me here to this moment.

I want to extend my gratitude to everyone willing to learn a bit more about my heart and your continued support of this unconventional way of being in the world. My hope is by sharing my journey, we can feel a little less alone in our experiences and dare to pursue our dreams—no matter how ambitious they may feel.

Most of all, I hope everyone has a chance to know someone as special as Jimmy Wolpert.

All my love,

Hayli Nicole

Jimmy

Your name
etched in stone
with a sort of permanence
my mind can't comprehend.
Your body
no longer an entity on this earth
yet I can still feel you
as if my arms are wrapped around you
and I am leaning into your chest
as I have always done.
I can't tell if the heart I hear beating
is that of my own
or if it's the echoes
of the one I deeply crave
in this permanent state of longing.
This...
Reality...
Is not real to me.
You are not gone
because in my mind
I committed to decades
filled with your laughter.
I didn't catalog it in my mind
all those times it filled the room
because those rooms
were always meant to be occupied
by us.
We never bought into goodbyes
because why would we ever acknowledge
the end to something so beautiful?
You are so beautiful.
Which makes this end so impossible to accept.
My heart screams in its sleep

for the man who gave me everything
and took it all away with his last breath.
The honest truth is
I died with you that day,
but in the light that is your love
I was revived.
You showed me the way
as you've done so many times before.
You opened the door
to a world I once again feared.
As I stepped through with your guidance
my path became clear.
I was lost but now I see
with certainty
I never strayed too far
from where you always wanted me to grow.
The earth quickly resumed its radiance
and allowed me to discover my own.
I found everything I was meant to become
all because you believed in me first.
The momentum of your loss
has carried me forward
in every encounter.
Every connection.
Every conversation.
Every smile is an extension of yours
though yours is the face
I wish I was staring back into
I see you in every living being
which is why it doesn't feel like you're gone.
As I move through this life
I know I will find you
beneath the shades of trees
and in the whispers of wind
and the turn of the Spring

when new life thrives and begins
to bring back the vividness
I remember life being
when you were still walking amongst us.
This life will get easier.
I will remember how to breathe.
The silence of the rooms you once filled
won't be so deafening.
This will definitely be
the hardest thing I have ever done,
but nothing was easy with you
which made everything worth it.
You are worth this
continued pursuit of brighter days
deeper love and richer experiences.
You gave me the world
and I promise to share that world with others
wrapped in the same gentle kindness
that overwhelms me
every time I hear
your name.

May 12, 1991 - June 12, 2018

Genesis

My Life is a Mess

My words so shaky.
My knees are weak.
My hand is unsteady.
My heart skips a beat.
My eyes start to shed.
My tears fall like rain.
My future's uncertain.
My heart full of pain.
My arms like spaghetti.
My mind filled with stress.
My thoughts are unclear.
My life is a mess.

Take It All In

"I wanted to live deep
and suck out the marrow of life."
-Henry David Thoreau

This world, the nature
their soothing words.
These simple messages
are all I've heard.

This sunlight, the birds
as they sing their love songs.
Welcomes this bliss
I've known all along.

This warmth, the life
that grows all around.
I tune into the symphony
of their peaceful sounds.

This shade, the breeze
flows over my skin.
I inhale, exhale
as I take it all in.

Broken Wings

I'm sitting all alone
in the darkened shadow.
I have seem to lost my way.

The wings She placed upon my back
have been broken in many places;
my freedom stripped before my eyes.

I want to fly away from the world
but the burden of other's pain
have been placed upon my wings.

I am unable to flee from this darkness.
Someday I will see the sun,
But it is not time to emerge quite yet.

I must learn to confront the pain
and wash my hands of the sorrow
to mend these broken wings
before I am free again.

Dreaming of Escape

The confidence,
diminished.
My comfort has been torn.
I hide the truth behind a smile
as the days become forlorn.
The happiness has faded
My eyes, they often weep.
I escape the consuming sadness
as I lay my head to sleep.
I slip into the darkness
and get lost behind my eyes
I fall into my dreams
to hide from the demise.
A slight outlook arises
when I lay here in the dark.
It's only me,
a thousand thoughts,
and the hope that's in my heart.
So, when I hit the pillow,
I know I'll be okay.
My dreams are here to save me
before I face another day.

Love Me, Winter

Simple whispers in the night
beckon the break of day.
A twirl, a jump, a delicate step,
carry these whispers away.
The shadows crawl through thick and thin,
and make their way to sight.
They play, they dance, they make new fun.
They vanish within the night.
A gentle touch brushes the sky
and strews a string of stars.
The rising moon evokes new love,
shining down on places far.
Behind the corner lurks the ghost;
a memory of lost time.
The whispers, shadows, and gentle touch,
are nothing more than mine.

Sober

A party beckons with beer and wine.
Provides impaired vision,
but I promise, not mine.
I'm steady and sober and willing to be
the designated driver.
I promise, that's me.
With keys in my hand,
I gather my friends
who reek of a stench
that's become a trend.
A calm drive home.
The drunks sound asleep.
The music stays soothing and I tip tap my feet.
But soon came a light.
So bright. So close.
Frozen in motion
as that bright light approached
With the turn of the wheel,
And a moment too soon,
My body now lies
under a crimson moon.
The cold swept over.
And in. And through.
My blood turned to ice.
My lips turned blue.
My skin turned pale
as I lay in the street.
And they shudder at youth
hidden under a sheet.
But I still stare deep,
no life, no breath.
at the woman who caused
my unfortunate death.

Drunk

A party beckons with beer and wine.
Provides impaired vision,
especially mine.
I wobble and slur and forget I will be
driving home later;
Drunk probably.
I scatter my purse,
I search for my coat,
and a, *Be careful, you're drunk,*
in a mental note.
A speedy drive home.
The wind. The rain.
I get lost in the music. I soar like a train.
I dropped my lighter
deep down between seats.
When I finally looked up,
I blared that loud beep.
With the turn of the wheel,
glass shattered and sprayed.
My hands kept on bleeding;
a small price I paid.
The cold swept over.
And in. And through.
My eyes turned to glaze.
My tears stayed blue.
I winced at the body
that lay in the streets.
I remembered that youth
as they laid down a sheet.
But I still stare deep
and with the loss of my breath
I was truly sorry
for causing her death.

Mothers of Mayhem

(Observations of the devastating
California fires of 2006)

Lush reds embellished trees
and whisked within the wind.
As flames of fury engulfed lives
Mother Mercy sought no end.

Brutal winds whirled the world
as embers were sent afloat.
The fires raged; the sky turned black.
Mother Faith had lost all hope.

The moon assumed the role of sun
igniting a midnight glow.
The flames continued to roll through hills,
but Mother Guidance let them grow.

As the physical life around us fell
lessons had been passed.
At the fate of the fire and flames
Mother Nature let her impressions last.

Ten Fallen Tears

One tear for the moment I tasted hate.
Two tears for the wretched outcome of fate.
Three tears for all the mistakes that I've made.
This is not the first time history has replayed.
Four tears for the laughs
and five for the pain.
Six for the kisses which barely remain.
My seventh tear is not saved for you,
but for that fact
that I stayed so true.
The eighth tear falls
when you question my embrace.
Nine is for the memories that time can not erase.
My tenth and final tear is my last goodbye.
Soon everything will pass,
and my ten tears will dry.

Constellations

Confide my trust in comfort of the night.
Beneath a blanket is where the sun lies.
And my fate is concealed by the moon light.
The constellations soar as they glide by.
The Leo, I see, courage is endowed.
By Cygnus the swan, sways her beauty's poise.
Orion the strength. Safety now allowed.
I choose to bask in silence of the noise.
Dear sun, arise with a chance to redeem.
And thou doth wakes with beauty in your rays.
The blanket tucked away—stars sleep to dream.
I watch as the mid night turns into day.
My pleasure vowed to the light of the stars
And at once my life seems to fade so far.

Kissed by a Rose

I choose to mask the red of lust that grows.
Beneath the petals lies my sacred love.
I prick my hand on thorns upon the rose,
Blood on skin, white as the whitest dove.
A beauty blooms with waking of the sun;
Revives the life that sleeps when night does fall.
The colors gleam as daylight has begun.
A morning dew now laces worlds so small.
And in the morning breeze the leaves do sway.
Now my faith doth floats onward to the creek.
And worries carry through and out; away.
It's all the messages I dare not speak.
But yet I see a new outlook on life.
A simple rose that represents love's strife.

Writer's Block

Loss of focus.
Lack of rhyme.
Losing energy.
Wasting time.
I can not write.
I will not speak.
Forgetting words.
Looking bleak.
Heightened feelings.
Weighted heart.
Searching. Scanning.
Failing art.
Missing flow.
Taking stock.
Desperate to break
this writer's block.

Writer's Block (Reprise 2019)

Sometimes the hardest thing as a writer
is the potential
of a blank page.
The voice in my head
is screaming to be put to paper,
but which words
are the right ones to preserve?
With limited lines
I must filter my mind,
but an edit means
I'm at war with those screams.
Anxiety grabs hold
and takes control
of the plume which remains
in idle hands.
I try to resume
the first stroke of ink,
but then I think
of the disappointment others
(especially my mother)
will have
in what I have to say.
This day
was supposed to be productive,
but in trying to produce art
I've fallen apart
reduced to a bag of what-ifs
I sit
still staring at the same blank page.
Maybe I'll try again tomorrow.

Love in Secrecy

Silent words,
a secret kiss.
With you I'm in a state of bliss.
Broken smile.
Open heart.
You keep me from falling apart.
No more tears;
the crying is done.
To me, you are the only one.
The moonlight's glow.
Internal flame.
If only you knew my name.

Celestial Waltz

Meet me in outer space tonight.
When the sun does fade, let life take flight.
Meet in the middle, half past moon.
I'm close behind. I'll be there soon.
We'll lose ourselves and strip our fears.
Journey distance in light-years.
I'll search for dreams cast through stars
and find my way back to your arms.
Indulge in planets rise past Earth.
Remain in bliss to see it first.
We'll freight the rings of ice in grace
and cherish time that has erased.
Our words defy the black abyss
for in our souls the stars persist.
In the still of silent space
we'll travel in our mind's embrace.
In reality we'll find
that to this beauty most are blind.
But this is where our true bond lays
and in the night our hearts will stay.
So, meet me in our realm tonight.
When the sun does fall, let us take flight.

Stay

I bear a heart that barely beats.
I tremor as nightmares repeat.
Haunted by mistakes I've made
realizing too late
I should have stayed.
The moment I chose to walk away
is the moment I'll regret
for the rest of my days.
If given another chance I would try
to show him all the reasons why.
Why I thought there was
something more than
the man I should have been fighting for.
Seeking a happiness I had yet to find
without realizing
it was already mine.
I wanted to see the world
and defy constraints,
but he had already allowed this
with no complaints.
He gave me the love I needed to grow;
the greatest gift one can bestow.
Instead of protecting his gracious heart,
I rendered our two worlds apart.
If allowed the chance
I'd want nothing more
than to be in the presence of the man I adore.
I'd wrap him in my arms
and kiss his lips.
Trace his cheek with fingertips.
Press my head to his chest,
record the beats so I'll never forget
the sound of a heart that once loved me whole.

The heart I would give anything to console.
I'd tell him I love him
just one more time
and assure him I know
the mistake was mine.
That if he'd give me the chance to fight,
I'd prove to him that he was right.
That our two souls were meant to meet
and his love is all I need to be complete.
For all that I've realized at second glance
I'd give my last breath
to have this chance.
For if I could take back that day,
I would do what I should have done.
I'd stay.

Growing Old

Light of day between the sheets
when hearts of two entwine and meet.
A bond pursues the unexplored
when broken paths are restored.
One heart finds its way to two
and in the silence they subdue.
Relinquish thoughts and then persist
in the moment that they exist
Lay in still of silent breath
and mourn as time nears its death.
When the hands stop one and five
the heart that stops remains alive.
Even when motions no longer stir,
love transcends when he finds her.

Goodbye

This may never touch a hand
or be seen with a single eye.
This is my final poem;
it contains my last goodbye.
This world that I grew up in
has been an act of lies.
People I once cared for
are now an object of despise.
I've had my share of heartache
and I've shed my share of tears.
You'll never feel the sorrow
I've endured through all these years.
The pain I've carried onward
has pushed me to the end.
So as you read this softly,
please pray my wounds will mend.

Foundations

Mother Earth

The soothing sound
of the swiftest streams
play the sound track of
our Mother's dreams.
Strength from her roots
lead to the skies.
Within her empire,
each life thrives.
Her breath, the wind.
Her heart, the sun.
On each exhale, they pulse as one.
Within these walls she forgives;
provides an equal chance to live.
Each being's life is bound as one.
The damage slowly comes undone.
We get to be.
To grow.
To die.
With each loss,
our Mother cries.
The rain escapes her teary eyes.
As she weeps she breathes new life.
I'm drawn to her.
    Her poise.
           Her grace.
I'm called to her;
drawn to this place.
My heart echoes her melodic call.
She is my mother.
She is all.

Mountain Meditations

I am here.
We are all.
Love in abundance.
Beauty in every shared breath.
Magic in this awakened state.
Seeing all as it is;
every sense alive.
The wind. The earth.
The here. Right now.
I feel the light pour through me;
fills me to the brim with hope
for a world awake
to finally see
what was always in front of us
and shall remain to be.

The Highlands

With rain-soaked skin
and tear stained cheeks.
I know my heart is here.
It is finally within reach.
In the embrace of the mountains
under a setting moon;
I never imagined for me
to find it so soon.
On the banks of a river
lined with polished stones
absorbing the warmth of the sun
the rare time it shows.
Or sitting beneath the shade
in a grove of sycamore trees
as clouds drift above us
in the gentle and soothing breeze.
I found it in the silence
between contentment and chilled breaths;
staring out over waters
of unknown origins and depths.
It was sitting by the fire
smitten by familiar songs sung new.
Writing beneath candlelight
huddled closely next to you.
In every glance across the room,
every sweet caress and craved kiss.
It was always there in your arms;
the sanctuary I deeply missed.
In the still of our last moments
I couldn't help but clearly see.
I found my heart where I left it,
when I finally returned to thee.

Someday

It has proven impossible to overcome
the distrust in the unknown.
An understandable place to be
despite the effort and affection shown.
To be in significantly different places,
both in the world and in our dreams,
is a disconnect we can't overcome
despite the volume at which our hearts scream.
I've known this place before—
the space between love and leaving.
I must ignore the urge to run towards you
for your heart is not meant for my own keeping.
I wish this could be our moment,
but to the truth I must give way.
Whether in this life or in the next,
I will always hold out hope for someday.

Cosmic Siren's Song

A song once fell upon my ears
carried distances by the wind
containing whispers of dreams cast to stars;
an eternal light which can't be dimmed.
A grand tale of a stellar being;
her impressions resonating on earth.
Her physical vessel a valued reminder
of our own evolution and rebirth.
Unaware of her own divinity
and the attention she commands,
she may be a woman of simple needs
but holds the world in her gentle hands.
Her infinite depths are reflected
in the layers of the setting sun.
Though beyond an object of desire,
she is the temptation to succumb.
A woman with her power
still embodies a distinct grace.
She moves through the world with intention;
no forward step misplaced.
She's loved a dozen darling hearts
and broken each one with her ways.
She's a perpetual leaver of places;
never inspired enough to stay.
The memory of her silhouette
lingers long after she's left.
She'll visit in your deepest slumber
and steal your every waking breath.
An encounter forever fleeting
of a spirit which cannot be tamed.
Her heart belongs to the cosmos which birthed her.
Her siren's song will be all that remains.

The Woman of the Sea

There is so much
beneath
the decks of this
weathered vessel.
I wonder how
she came to be.
How long has it taken
for her maiden voyage
to lead her here?
What kind of
wreckage
floats in the
ripples
of those chestnut eyes?
What is hidden
beyond the shores,
remaining undiscovered
in the vast sea
that is her mind?
What I would give
to get carried away
in the currents
of her thoughts
and drift to sleep
in the stillness
of her heart.

I'll Call Him Weeds

Oh, to see the world through his eyes;
Standing barefoot at the edge
of the world
embracing the wildness
within the nothingness.
Oh, to retrace his steps
through this life and the dozens past,
staring into the vastness
of this existence
and understanding our place
within it all.
His eyes,
his mind,
call to me.
I've never seen them before,
yet I recognized them
in this place immediately.
Our space in time
so perfectly aligned
on the banks of the Trinity River.
I, his Smoky Stranger.
Him, the seeds that
rooted in my heart
on this day
and grow as rampant and wild
as the wilderness in front of us.
I don't remember his name,
so I'll just call him Weeds.

The People You Meet and the Trouble You Get Up To

I've never been one to linger
in dark corners of bars
with people I've just recently met.
But the company we keep
in these early hours
are connections I'm not willing to forget.
We befriended these strangers,
our curiosity being
the stories of their leisure.
When you're wild in the world
you meet interesting people
doing interesting things with their lives.
They invite you into their sphere
and share with you a glimpse
of how you all came to arrive.
It's curious.
Why is it our paths
were the ones to align
when so many others could arrive
at this same moment?
Of all the directions we could have gone,
how did we all follow the same one
to arrive here
on this night,
together?
There is an assumption
travellers are running from something
but I find we are running
towards the same thing.
We have dreams
which reach farther
than our western roots will allow.

We chase borders,
not build them,
for we understand
there is nothing to fear beyond them.
We want the same chances for others
as we've had for ourselves
because there is nothing more beautiful
than the world growing together
in perfect unison,
harmony, and prosperity.
The similarity
is striking.
Even if our tongues have memorized
different words and their signs.
Words aren't the thread
binding their journey to mine.
Love is the only thing
standing between
our collective experience
and our reason for remaining
in this room
causing a ruckus,
together.
So we sit around playing Jenga
with the self-proclaimed gypsies
drumming along
to the French songs they sing.
We fall in love with their kindness
while finding surprise
in the stories responsible for their being.
We drink warm beers
and smoke rolled cigarettes,
whispering our regrets to the night.
Our plights
far too similar,

but here it doesn't define
the content of our character
the way it did
in the places we left behind.
From the outside,
they looked like trouble,
but the trouble we're in
is no trouble at all
when the conversation is free
and our once guarded hearts are open.
We fall into trouble
because it's a safe place to be
when surrounded by people
who feel and think
and move through the world
just like us.
Maybe the trouble is
it took too long
to end up where
we needed to land.
Amongst friends
we were always meant to call ours.
Still lurking in the shadows
of a bar
we had no intention being in.
When we finally retreat,
we walk beneath the full moon
reminiscing about the joy
and absurdity of the night's end.
The trouble, now,
is the long journey home
with no promise of finding
trouble like this again.

Natural State of Being

The dark, the night, the calm, the still,
provide a warmth blood can not fill.
The beats repeat beneath skin.
I hold you close, I let you in.
Warm and soft, your skin on mine
creates bliss when worlds entwine.
Your blood, my blood fuse to one.
Nerve ends fray I come undone.
As the blanket molds to bones,
your pulse defies all that I've known.
All senses cut off at the spine,
enthralled with lust, your lips meet mine.
I lay exposed.
Here.
Heart and soul.
Short of the breath that you have stole.
At the mercy of your grace,
our spirits waltz in silent space.
Our bodies may meet and grow as two,
but you are me and I am you.

The Wild Woman

She flounces around
in sequins and fringe.
She trusts in the tarot
for questions she seeks within.
She dances bare naked
under the harvest moon.
Its white glow shrouds her skin
in a tender cocoon.
She is attuned to the energy
of all living beings
using crystals as guidance
for universal meanings.
She knows nothing else
than her role as a giver
for her faith is in the cosmos
which endlessly deliver.
She is a perpetual dreamer
who sees beyond stars;
no opportunity too vast
to one day call hers.
She whispers dreams into darkness
knowing they will see the light
and with them her gratitude
for her earthly plight.
She moves with intention
through foreign lands.
The deeper connections she makes,
the further her mind expands.
Her head on a swivel,
her heart in surrender.
She lives in abundance
of life's beauty and splendor.
There are few enraged battles

she is willing to fight
for love will always fill
her beacon of light.
Her grace extends to all
under the same rising flame.
The zest of her spirit
never meant to be contained.
She is the force of the oceans,
every quake of the earth.
She is the strength in the roots
which foster nature's rebirth.
Drawn by her magnetism
we discover guides and sages.
Women bettering the world
through shared wisdom of the ages.
With her light as our guidance,
our earthly vessels align.
Our fierce femininity
a reflection of the divine.
As we unearth our own potential
in her presence we will thrive.
For the wild woman was always within us,
and forever she remains alive.

Shwedagon (Yangon)

Under the shade of the Bodhi,
I shallow my breath.
As life stirs around me,
in stillness, I am kept.
I surrender to vibrations.
The commotion.
The chimes.
Entranced by the senses,
in that same stillness I rise.
My heart beats in tune
with the sound of the birds.
A near perfect unison
of every melody heard.
I waltz in the light
and sway with the leaves.
Revel in the universe
and the intricacies it weaves.
What lies within is reflected
in the world around.
Relinquishing perception,
I am no longer bound.
The distant gongs ringing
returns me here.
Without exploring the questions,
all solutions appear.
To deny this connection
is to ignore my fate.
With clarity I see love
(and life) to create.
Wrapped in the cool
whirl of the wind,
under the shade of the Bodhi,
my journey begins.

Under the Burmese Sun

It was him.
Engaged with the world I so deeply love.
Seeing it pass exactly as I.
Drawn by his eyes,
a warmth and kindness
any stranger would want
to be invited into.
Yet it was I
he graciously invited into his world.
I was eager to explore its horizons.
I yearned for his heart
beating with mine
as we embraced for the first time.
My bones are still tingling.
His soft sighs
from parted lips fell upon my ears
and pulled me in further with every breath.
A shared stillness
yet a silence that screams louder than
any truth I have ever known.
Our fleeting love.
His was the heart I was searching the world for.
I found it here,
under the Burmese sun,
exactly where I left mine to begin with.

Distant Longing

Distance divided lovers' hearts
while worlds away; oceans apart.
A lonely life when lived alone.
My counterpart is unbeknown
of just how much I yearn—I miss
the tenderness of lover's kiss.
I miss the warmth of smiling eyes
and how much love one look implies.
My greatest fears his heart enfolds.
His gentle touch renders me whole.
His words soothe my troubled mind;
always patient, never unkind.
His is my light in the darkest days;
following his heart when I've lost my way.
With each beat, he draws me in.
This path will always lead back to him.
I've searched this world to find my place,
but I've found my home in his embrace.
I dream of the day we finally meet
for my heart and my world will be complete.
Though we're in this war with time,
I am forever his and he is mine.

He

He came out of nowhere—
like a comet entering the atmosphere
burning with the heat
and radiance of a thousand suns.
I surrendered to the pull of his uncontainable energy.
Who is this celestial being?
With his green and blue eyes with gold
that glisten in the light of the full moon
on the steps of Montmartre.
He moves with such ease and grace
it is as if he's walked this earth
over the span of a dozen lives.
Our energies have done this dance before.
I have felt him in every beat of my heart
since the day I became aware of it beating.
Every breath belongs to him.
Oh, to be his now.
I will follow him
wherever his dreams may lead
and if we must be apart
I will find him in the world
again and again and again.
Because falling into his arms
is like returning home
after he set my wandering soul free in the world
far longer than I was meant to be gone.
I love it.
I love him.
I love you (Je t'aime).
The wild man I've searched the galaxy for.

Emergence

Hanging on to his words
under Yangon skies.
The next thing he says
will be the timely demise
of the fear that once lived
in my fragmented soul
for his tender caress
renders my heart whole.
Let this be the death of the notion
I'm unworthy of this:
the abundance of his love
and to be deeply missed.
Let this end the resistance
to a new lover's touch
and numbing myself
as a temporary crutch.
For as I collapse in his arms
he dissolves all the fear
from the burden of trauma
I've trudged all these years.
Let this be the closure
of the darkest stage of my life
and realizing my full potential
in the radiance of his light.
To hear his heart beating
is all the hope I need
to step boldly into the future
and set my wild spirit free.

Émergence

Accrochant à ses mots
sous les cieux de Yangon.
La prochaine chose qu'il dit
sera la disparition déplacée
de la peur qui vivait une fois
dans mon âme fragmentée
car sa tendre caresse
rend mon cœur entier.
Que ce soit la mort de la notion
je suis indigne de ceci:
l'abondance de son amour
et d'être profondément manqué.
Que cela termine la résistance
au contact d'un nouvel amant
et l'insensibilité émotive
comme une béquille temporaire.
Car comme je m'effondrais dans ses bras
il a dissous toute la peur
du fardeau du traumatisme
j'ai traversé péniblement toutes ces années.
Que ceci soit la conclusion
de l'étape la plus sombre de ma vie
et de réaliser mon plein potentiel
dans l'éclat de sa lumière.
Entendre les battements de son coeur
est tout l'espoir dont j'ai besoin
de me lancer intrépidement dans l'avenir
et libérer mon esprit sauvage.

Emergence

Gems in Human Form

I explore the depths
of his earthly being.
Each question
a calculated excavation
of his knowledge,
insight, and opinions.
Slowly unearthing the parts
he often keeps buried.
I find treasure
in the gems
of the experiences
he deems worthy
to be held
in curious hands.
I trace the facets
of his polished exterior
knowing the time it took
to shape the rugged origins
into the beauty
I am now able to inspect.
I hold his raw form
in the same adoration
but it's the process of transforming
which captivates
my deepest respect.
I hold all parts of him
in the same regard
before returning him
to the place in the world
we both found ourselves to be.
Our being mirrored
in the reflections of
each other's polished brilliance.

Esalen

I arrived in the dark
but I was seen
immediately
by people I had never seen before.
Not even the cloak of night
could keep me
concealed from the curiosity
of these kind strangers.
I lingered in the corner
waiting to be the last
to strip down to bare bones
and cleanse my shame
before immersing in
the healing springs
and the conversations to come
from our being there.
Squirming in my nakedness
I wondered
how much of my discomfort
was mine to bear.
My bones trembled
until the warmth of the waters
swallowed my nipples.
My shoulders
relinquished the burden
of objectification
and fell naturally into place
free from the years
of their conditioning.
The moonless sky
allowed the stars to shine
in all their full intensity.
The sheen on my breasts

a cosmic glistening
among the rippling of the water.
Our bodies shifting
where the cold of the air
met the heat of the spring.
My being was re-birthed
in the safe space
held by strangers
bathing naked in the night
on the cliff's edge
high above the sea
with the endless universe
above us.

France

These mornings;
steam rising from stained mugs
warming bones.
In the dew that clings to leaves
my reflection in the beads
of yesterday's rain.
With outstretched arms
I drink in the grey sky.
No gloom can take away my sun.
Not this morning.
Not today.

Love in London

These precious moments
when he reaches
for my hand
and I fall into his arms
and we watch the light
ignite the clouds
through the window
somewhere between
Camden and Stanmore.
I don't know
what feels better;
the scruff of his beard
against my bare cheek,
the puffs of his breath
against my neck
in perfect unison with
the rise and fall
of my own chest,
or his gentle kisses
under the setting sun.
These are some
of my favorite things
to come from
the turning of spring
and these lovely days in London.

Wild Atlantic Way

Rolling hills of green wonder
stretch endlessly
as far as my curious eyes can see.
I trace their lines
with floating fingers
outside my window
catching the wind of our momentum
in the palm
of my outstretched hand.
Steady tones
of the clearest skies
mirror the turquoise waters.
The clouds hang
in clean straight lines
like a blanket snug against the shore.
Each bend of the road
reveals more
than what I knew
mere moments before this second.
My heart feels the most open
when I let the open road
lead me
to all the beautiful places
I have yet to know.
The world is waiting;
calling me by name,
reminding me of the freedom
that awaits
in my finally leaving.

Chain Smoking I

Maybe I never told you,
but you're the reason
I fell in love with the road.
You're to blame for
all these years I've been gone,
but now you are
the hardest part of leaving.
I see your age revealing itself more
in the lines on your face.
The chunk missing from your nose
a reminder of the wars waged
for your health.
Always in high spirits,
and jest,
you're ageless to me,
but I always wished
we had found each other sooner.
We didn't have a relationship back then
though my self-centeredness
may have been to blame.
It was the same time
my family had fallen apart.
I wasn't eating
and I think you saw me
fading away
into the same nothingness
as the broken home
I didn't ask to be in.
So the day you asked me
to drive across the country
I knew it was my only
chance to escape.
Your Honda Fit became

a new symbol for freedom
and we started our journey
across the south to Venice.
I had never seen the Gulf Coast
but I was in the business
of seeing something new
if it meant leaving
everything behind.
I counted cigarettes
instead of miles
because you were like a chimney
billowing into the desert sky.
I made fleeting friends
with the saguaros
passing outside my window
naming them
as I quickly sketched
their contorted figures
to keep me from going insane.
Somewhere under the stars in Texas
you called blown tires, *gators,*
because they will rip you to shreds.
I remember rest stops
were respite from the dread
of plowing through
another blurred landscape.
It took under three days,
constant naps for me
but no sleep for you,
and 48 cigarettes
to reach Florida.
I don't remember why
but you said to me,
"It's not the destination,
it's the adventure to get there."

Sage wisdom from the man
who wore a hat which read,
"Different Day,
Same Old Bullshit."
I scribbled your words under
Cigarette #50.
I wouldn't understand
the depth of the wisdom
you imparted until years later
when I was stranded
smoking cigarettes
next to a motorbike
with an empty tank
somewhere in the highlands
of Vietnam.
This road was leading me
even further from home
but my mind was
on the porch swing
of your brother's house
sitting next to you.
It was after Christmas
but before the New Year.
We were listening to the rain
and I was imagining a life
I never thought
I would claim as mine.
I wrote:
Ride a Motorbike Through Vietnam
under:
Publish a Book
because even at eighteen,
I wanted freedom to mean
more than a red car
driving towards a rising sun.

It took almost ten years
for them to take shape,
but you were there
sitting silently,
lighting another cigarette
while I lit the flame
to ignite my dreams.
That was the day
I wrote into existence
the life I'm currently living.
Which is why the smell of Marlboro
always reminds me of you;
in those days
we were bathing in it,
often silent,
but together.
I didn't know it then,
but chain smoking
became synonymous with
my first taste of freedom
and my grand adventure
across the country
with the greatest grandpa
who ever lived.

Chain Smoking II

I never smoke cigarettes
until I needed a reason
to remain silent
surrounded by a language
I only partially understand.
Sifting through words
like a room
clouded with smoke.
I choked on my reply.
Maybe they won't
question my silence
if I ask them for
another light.

Chain Smoking III

The weight of leaving
hanging in my throat,
burning
like the cigarette
in parted lips
keeping me
from the speaking
the emotions
that can only mean
Goodbye.

Between the Sun and the Tides

On the shores of sadness
the spectrum of our experiences
are carried in
the rise and fall
of the tides
we have yet to understand.
They come and they go
as we remain still
staring out
over open waters
eager to be
the sun shining
in full intensity;
unafraid of the horizon
it's about to descend
knowing the depths
it must see
before rising
into an open sky
to resume its radiance.
Casting its glow
over turbulent waters,
I wonder if the sun knows
the intensity of colors
it leaves behind
each time it retreats.
Still depleted,
I want to know
if my colors show
the spectrum within my heart
instead of reflecting
the greys of the all the storms
I've endured.

Presence is...

… an early rise with tired bodies
piling into a car with a stranger.
It's back roads and sharp curves
leading us to our destination.
Flickering lights in freezing palms
illuminating well-trodden paths.
The shuffle of bodies
and the rising of voices
means we're no longer alone
in the night.
Scree covered trails in the dark means
the crunching of earth
under boots broken in
by our previous climbs.
It's taking time to admire the stars
because from up here
they're never too far away.
It's Rinjani half covered in the distance
by the morning haze
while a red sun burns
from somewhere behind it
casting colors on the clouds
only the first break of day could create.
It's warm coffee
cupped in still cold hands
waiting for the warmth of the sun
to swallow our bodies whole.
It's gold hues reflected on the ocean
just beyond the ridge line
reminding us of our place
between heaven and earth
and the worth of our being present.

Overboard

Once I lost a poem
to the ocean.
It came to me
in a dream on a boat
floating idle under the Milky Way.
It was a few days after a full moon
and nothing terrible had gone wrong.
So when it was carried overboard
by the wind into the sea,
I cursed the moon
for the chaos it brings
and for stealing words
from my hands
without warning.
I wondered if I could
rewrite what was written
but I knew the words
wouldn't be the same.
The feeling was different now;
blanketed by regret
for not keeping them safe
to begin with.
I tried to imagine them
into a new existence
before the ink
bled into nothing
but it's impossible
to replicate creativity
pouring through
scribbling hands.
For poetry flows
like swift currents
past untouched beaches

on islands unoccupied by man.
Poetry is in the sand
churned out through time
taking different forms
so far from its original shape
it is no longer the coral
or the shells,
or the rocks,
it once was,
but a grain
in a magnificent landscape
shaped by the movement of water.
Nothing could compare
to the rising of tides
inspired by the moon
and worshiped through time
as the giver of life.
So when the sea
swallowed my words
I didn't feel worthy.
For the ocean is the poem
I could never write
into existence
even if I tried.

In Idle Waters

A world waking up
is the engine of
a fishing boat
sputtering past
where we drift.
A rift in the stillness
sending ripples
from its subtle wake.
The dawn breaking soon,
but first shrouding the waters
in a pastel hue
and revealing more
of the mountains
which surround us
in waiting
under a partial moon
for the day to arrive.
I shallow my breath
to hold onto the silence
a moment longer
knowing these are
our final moments
waking up as one
with the sea.

Sumatra

The dawn's rays
through parted leaves
revealing
life under the canopy
of the rainforest.
A spider's trail
glistens silver in the sun.
Birds calling out,
but not to each other.
The river runs past
where I've bathed in naked silence
the last two days
as smoke from camp
holds a veil to the sky.
The stones will soon be dry
leaving no trace of last night's rain
except in the earth
held damp by a blanket
of fallen leaves.
Time is of irrelevance
when everything exists
simultaneously.
And in the nothingness
I hear the echoes
of a long call
bringing me back
to this moment
of surrender.

Mundane Musings

Is it possible to have seen
the sky so many times
you no longer see it
for what it is?
Because I see a canvas,
for the sun and the clouds
to paint a million masterpieces
by never replicating
the same techniques.
I was told my whole life
the sky is blue
but the most beautiful skies
I have ever seen
are every shade
except for the color of sadness.

I've watched barren fields
become home to super blooms
of flowers as wild as my soul.
When fragrance fills the space
where the chill
of winter once lived
I can't help but think
of all the times
he bought my favorite bouquet
to fill our home
with the scent of Spring.
Have you ever seen
a field of flowers so beautiful
you forget the heart
broken by the person
who promised
to protect it?

It's become impossible for me
to see the ocean
and not weep.
Because sea salt spraying
from the crashing of waves
reminds me of all
the days I spent
driving up the coast
in search of something more.
The California shore
always felt like freedom.
And when I listen to the sea
I hear every song
echoing
from the mixed tape
I played in my '86 Chevy Caprice
and all the boys I kissed
in the back seat of that
blue tufted velvet interior.
Kissing boys
meant becoming a woman
and the ocean is every reminder
of the woman
(and force of nature)
I have become.

I have found bliss in the shade
of trees I know not the names of.
Seeking shelter in the chill
of their cover,
tickled by the grass
cut fresh after a summer rain.
There is joy in a hummingbird
drinking sweet nectar
while suspended in perfect balance.

Its wings fluttering
at the speed of my thoughts,
but bringing stillness to the moment.
Happiness is the sound of a wind chime
dancing in the breeze
of a day ending.
It's spending time drinking coffee
in a mug gifted by a friend
and with each sip
tasting the memories
of better days spent in their presence.

Sometimes I smile
for no other reason
than the simplicity of a moment.
Maybe I see the beauty
in too many things
and I bare my emotions
the entire length of my sleeve,
but I know what it means
to live in the shadows
somewhere between black and grey.
Which is why I am no longer afraid
to leave what's familiar
in pursuit of
the unknown.
I was blinded by the veil
of my conditioning
so when I began to see
the sky and the flowers
and the sea again,
I remembered all the wonderful things
that used to fill my head
and I lived there
instead of staying.

I became the dandelion
growing through the cracks
of some else's foundation
in search of the sun.
My growth was unstoppable
and I outgrew the restraints
restricting my being and
keeping me in a place
of complacency.

From the rubble of
the life I dismantled,
I built sandcastles
and returned home to the ocean
under cotton candy skies.
I picked my favorite flowers
and released them in the water,
releasing all the loves I've known
who made me question
my perception of beauty.
And with the forgiveness
I vowed to never again become
blind to the magic
of the mundane.
Because if these little moments
can breathe inspiration
into depleted lungs,
imagine the magnificence
that will come
from never needing permission
to chase beauty in
the world again.

Therapy

I tried to remember
how many times
I climbed
these flights of stairs
and entered this same room
to pour the words
stored in my mind
through the falling of tears.
Like a puddle,
I collapsed in surrender
to how fragmented my life had become.
Holding the shards of what was
in pleading hands
I begged,
"Help me understand
how to be whole."
All I asked was for my soul
to be free
to wander to corners
inspired by my curiosity.
I didn't mean
to dismantle the love
we promised
would always be ours.
How far must I go
to show you
this has nothing to do
with your ways of seeing,
but instead was a fight
for my own well-being?
I wasn't fleeing
the life we intended to build.
I was freeing

my heart to be wild in the world.
We sat on the edges
of the same room
protected
by our narratives
unwilling to emerge
the beautiful ones we were
when this all began.
How can we mend
when we've retreated
behind our defenses,
relentlessly
blaming each other
for mistakes
easily prevented?
This safe space
we entered
was supposed to answer
how to mend
what was broken.
Our love was supposed to be
the one thing
we had going for us,
but not even love
could save
what little was left of us
in the end.

Rewriting Our Endings

I've flipped through the pages
of our love story a million times.
I committed our ending to memory
without ever reading our story to the end.
We uttered the words, "Happily ever after,"
but we are the lead characters
in a tragedy of our own making.
We promised forever,
but fairy tales
never end the way you want them to.
We believed we were on different chapters
of the same story,
but it turns out
we were never writing the same book.
My adventure is somewhere
in an encyclopedia under Nomadic
and yours is under
Business Strategy and Management.
While one can try to understand the other
or stories were never meant to coincide.
Even Dewey's Decimals say
we are on opposite ends of the classification.
Though our books are able to sit on the same shelf,
our worlds were defined by different parameters.
Our different ways of believing
meant different directions in living.
Those directions
were never as aligned as they seemed.
Since the day I discovered
a boundless mind
I've imagined worlds beyond the cosmos
where swinging on vines is the norm
and it's ritual to dance naked

under the seven moons.
I've always known comets
were never meant to be captured
in the same way some creatures
were never meant to be tamed.
It turns out,
I am the comet.
I am the creature.
I was always meant to be wild in the world,
but I gave all that up for you.
I abandoned my ways of being
to make you comfortable in yours,
but by being in yours
we neglected the ending
that was always meant to be mine.
It was left unwritten.
Out of sight,
gathering dust on the shelf
where you left me behind.
The critics destroyed me
while they sang your praises
and somewhere your story
became more important than
anything I had to say.
I remained hidden in the shadows
writing long into the night
pouring my heart out
to fill your pages
with no attention given to my own.
I handed you the Cliff Notes
but I could see
you weren't really living
in the world
you were relying on me to create.
Detached from the narratives

of the characters around us,
you were only concerned
about your personal gain
in the grand adventure.
Your logical mind puts price tags on creativity
because survival was always
a six-figure investment
in an empty existence.
I tried to help rewrite your ending
and show you the worlds waiting
beyond those stagnant shelves.
You skimmed the pages,
but you weren't willing to explore
the stories bridging my world and yours.
I found myself a Thousand Leagues Under the Sea,
but you prefer to breathe at the surface
and wade in the shallows
than descending to depths
I'm eager to understand.
I burrowed under blankets
with a light illuminating these pages
wanting to read with you
the greatest story ever written,
but you told me to stop being silly.
I traded in Fantasies for Self-Help
because you made me believe
it was the only way I could belong.
Like a mermaid
in a concrete jungle
I drowned trying to grow feet from fins.
My wildness was a spectacle
but never respected
and I carried the burden
of never belonging in
the places we've occupied together.

It took me time, but I realized
the only burden I'm meant to carry
is the weight of the world
in the physical books
written by the dreamers
who inspired my own dreams.
The same books which will one day
fill the shelves of my home
facing the sea.
Their spines never collecting dust,
but reminding me of the horizons
I have yet to explore
and the characters
I'm eager to share those horizons with.
Which is why I have to set myself free.
Not only to see where your story leads,
but to finish writing the ending to my own.
I need you to understand
one day my story will hopefully land
on the shelves amongst legends
which will inspire the next wave
of dreamers such as myself.
Dreamers who will open their hearts
to life's possibilities
and write hopeful endings
for a brighter future.
All I desire is to be free in my world
the way you've been so free in yours.
So that ripples from our shared tears
over the fairy tale ending that was lost
can transform into waves
and lead us to the shore
of the endings
we both deserve.

Dearest Dublin

I remember our first crisp morning together.
Tangled sheets
cocooned my jet lagged body.
I allowed the warmth to swallow
my being whole.
The skies were blue,
but it was the beginning of spring.
I had never heard birds sing
as if they were praising
the presence of the sun.
Their whistles were the soundtrack
to our first days of being home.
There was a nip at the neck
distinct in its stinging.
My California blood was still warm
but not warm enough
to keep me from freezing.
We were like two lovers
leaning into each other,
learning this new land
with pinch me, we're dreaming smiles.
For miles
we followed the river
weaving our way through the city.
We were pretty certain this is what
happiness looked like.
Our hands intertwined
dreaming of what our days would become.
We had no knowledge
our new home
would be the demise of our love.
See.
In seeking your shelter

I lay roots
in faulty foundations.
Your appeal
was promising
but the yield was never as promised.
I never found
what you said I would find.
Your patterns unkind,
you left me in the dark.
assuming I could pull myself
from the depression
of your constant grays.
So many days were spent
dreaming of how to escape.
I traced your silhouette
with the gentle hands of a new lover
I knew the intricacies
of your every corner,
but our intimacy
was only one way.
I remember the day I discovered another love.
I was somewhere under the Burmese sun
and you were here
promising you had begun
to change your ways.
So I came home
to you,
but something within me
was different now
and there was no going back for us.
It rained the day we decided to end.
Like every feeling I had been burying inside
burst through a wide-open sky
and poured over me
like the first time

I felt the sea meet my skin.
I couldn't tell
if the wetness of my cheeks
was that of the rain
or the pain
of not seeing this coming.
I retraced those first steps along the canal
leading me straight home.
I combed through memories
collecting pieces of the shattered past
trying to piece together
the bigger picture
all the while
wondering where it all went wrong.
This was meant to be my grandest love,
but love doesn't live where it used to.
It's winter's arrival
and I will be returning
to lands unfamiliar.
My heart is yearning to stay
than return to the pace of life
unbeknown to me now.
It seemed as though
we had more time.
Was it really two years?
Or was it a mirage within a dream
I'm struggling to wake myself from?
Everything feels lucid
but you never did
feel like the real thing.
The shade feels colder now,
but the sky the same blue.
The frost of the winter is making room
for new blooms
to breathe life

into the grey mornings again.
Except I won't be here to inhale
the scent of a city being reborn.
It's strange
how I haven't even left,
but already I see you changing
as if my presence
was of insignificance
because a new lover
will soon take my place
if they haven't already.
The season of change is upon us
pulling us back in the directions
we were meant to be heading.
I've been dreading this goodbye,
my dearest Dublin,
but if there's one thing I've learned,
my dear,
all beautiful things
must come to an end.

Hayli Nicole is a poet, travel writer, and photographer.

While her roots are in San Diego, she has found homes in the hearts of people in communities around the world. Her nomadic way of living has inspired deep soul connections while immersing in cultures and seeking the common threads of our human experience. Her greatest muse is love, though she finds plenty of inspiration in the mundane to stoke the fires of her creativity and imagination. There is always a story to be found, heard, cherished, and told. The ocean is her life source, but the mountains are regularly calling her to seek silence and solitude under the stars.

When she's not scribbling away in a journal, you can find her showering her friends in love and hugs, browsing flea markets and used book stores, observing orangutans at the San Diego Zoo, performing spoken word, attending comedy shows, drinking craft beer, or making friends with a stranger in the corner of a small cafe.

You can follow her everyday musings on Instagram @haylicans or see what adventure she is up to next on www.haylinicole.com.

www.ingramcontent.com/pod-product-compliance
Lightning Source LLC
Chambersburg PA
CBHW060359050426
42449CB00009B/1813